DIDACTIC DOPAMINE
THE COLLECTION

A poetic novel

by

Phyl▪liz Sóph°i▪kăl
the Phonetician

Copyright © 2013 by Phylliz Sophikal
(Whitney S. Boyd-Edwards). All rights reserved.

No part of this publication may be reproduced, stored in a retrieval system, or transmitted in any way or by any means electronic, mechanical, photocopying, recording, or otherwise without prior written permission of the copyright holder. May be used in the case of brief quotations embodied in critical articles and reviews.

All material written by Whitney S. Boyd-Edwards

Book format and design by Whitney S. Boyd-Edwards

Cover Graphics and Design by Maurice Thompson
    for Clickartist Media

Edited by Whitney S. Boyd-Edwards
    Associate Editor: Joseph Cox III
    Consultant Editor: Lawrence J. Dandridge

ISBN-13   978-0-9899273-9-0
ISBN-10   0989927393

Printed in the United States of America

In Dedication...

To the power of the legacy that I have inherited from my Ancestors.

To Hip-Hop Headz everywhere.

To Mama Jetta, for your unfailing love and support through this journey.

To children of color who have a dream - **Believe in it,** and do not stop until it is fully realized.

I give thanks for you...

Acknowledgements

I celebrate and give thanks for...

The Grace and Mercy of the Most High.

All of my Guardian Angels & Ancestor-Angels.

My daughter, my Divine reflection.

My family, extended family, & kindred spirits who continue to support my efforts, achievements, & visions.

The late Legendary Jan Carew, who helped me to remember the responsibility that comes with Our gifts, and encouraged me to actively create my reality.

To Copper John, who constantly reminded me of the importance of one's destiny and legacy.
Rest in peace, brother.

To Yayi Mbele, for being a voice of reason and wisdom and helping guide me to Greatness.

Mentors, whose various investments in me will never be forgotten or underappreciated.

Didactic Dopamine
The Collection

Track List

Episode 1:

Jupiter Eyes.............................7
Papyrus: Because Your Watercolors
    Move Me......................11
Excavated Treasures..................14
I Call You Zen...........................16
Marco Polo..............................19
Pretty Pictures..........................23
I Just Want You to Know:
    A Tangential Romantic
        Epithet..............25
aSankofaTypaLuv: OurStory..........29
Oracle and Warrior
    (aSankofaTypaLuvPt.II)....31

Episode 2:

Enter-mission..........................37
Stripper Culture: Dancin' for
    Dingy Dollars................38
Institutional Prostitution
    (Reflections of a Strange
        Bed-Fellow)...................41
Pipe Dreams............................44
Calamine Lotion: Mama, the Bumps
    Don't Itch No Mo'............48
Letter from a Concerned
    "Citizen".......................52
Left to Write............................57
Reflections on Lyrical Alchemy
    (For Hip-Hop Headz
        Everywhere).................58
She Was God:
    An Ode to Hip-Hop.........62

Episode 3:

He Compared Me to Water.........67
Cobwebs: An Unprecedented
    Love Affair....................70
A Long-Distance Love-Mesh.......72
Where I *Cum* From..................75
An Ethereal Threesome 78
She's Infatuated with Satin..........81
Love Harder..............................84

Episode 4:

Surrender................................87
Retribution through Rebirth.........90
La Brea: In Reverence of the
    Souls at Pitch Lake...........92
Because War, Too, is Sacred.......94
In the Center of My Lotus...........96
I Am Balance: A Meditation.........99
First Poem in Dedication to *you*...102
Daughter of Two Mothers.........103
Dedicated to the Big Bang.........104

Episode 1:

"My Dear, my dear, my dear,
you do not know me,
but I know you very well,
  Now let me tell you
  about the feelings I have
  for you…"

— PASSIN ME BY PHARCYDE
(1993)

Jupiter Eyes

She remembers him fondly,
And gives thanks for the gentle breeze
that brought forth the blessing that was him.

Jupiter Eyes,

  I will never forget
                       Interplanetary
                       travel with you,

And the quantum singularities that engulfed us
                        in the midst of conversation.

Pluto and Mars don't seem so far
Until interlocking webs and juxtaposed palms are
       no longer feasible.
So forgive my clammy,
               Un-companioned hands
               that wring with anxiety
'Cause they don't know any better,
And all they have is each other...
               Something I can't say was ever true for you
     and I.
But beauty recognizes beauty,
And light merges *infinitely* with light...

And we have come together to create rays of violet
That penetrate the gray scales in our Spirits.

I remember your love like acid
                    r
                     a
                     i
                     n,
Toxic purity to stain my clothes and
        my unempathetic memories.

You exist in the bowels of my spirit,
The seat of my soul,
The drum that resides in my ear,
 and **echoes** through my chest...
If you can still faintly hear the song that you composed,
I will know that you have not yet forgotten
The scent of mangoes
                            at midnight,
         Complimentary
         forehead kisses,
                    Brown-stew chicken and a side of
                    Caramel thunder...
Perfect lighting
So the moon captures the
shadows in your dimples just right.
A portrait of **para-perfection**,
The image of your lips pursed courageously
against mine
Continues to breech   the   gap
of my corpus collosum.
And if I am brave enough to think of you in the daytime,
Then I should do so in a place
where thunderstorms may readily occur within my Spirit,
And I can scream thanks to YEYE OSHUN
For allowing me to experience
                       a love like
             ***honey, cinnamon*, and
             sweet citrus.**
Know that when dawn breaks,
And Yansa whispers gently in my ear through cracks in the
windows,
    I
    AM
    REMEMBERING
    YOU,
Being sure to take a few moments to honor
The Manifestation of *Providence*
And a love so rare that Cupid had to
                          re-strategize
                          his game plan.

I welcome you back into my sacred space thru solemn recollections,
And if you find yourself hangin' around Saturn soon,
I'd be delighted to play horseshoe with you,
Patty-cake with the grown little girl that loves you,
And re-embody child-like innocence.
                        Our interaction
                        re-defines intimacy,
                        For I have not *known* you Biblically,
                                  But forgive me for
                                        climaxxin' out of turn…

Being *understood* is the pinnacle of sexual satisfaction,

And being *appreciated* is like
                        being
                            held after.

I remember the scent of intellectual seduction,
        Smells sumthin' like Citronella Oil and curry potatoes.
        The sweet music of your mind
        Distracted me from mosquitoes
        And fulfilled the empty corners of my stomach.
I am well, but I can't help wanting to reach into the past,
Take your hand, and bring you forward
Into a reality that feels like a bed
                            of
                            sun-flowers
                            and toes tickling the
                            water's edge.

            We can dro
                    w
                          n in the Caribbean Sea
Of our strongest desires and amorous endeavors…

Jupiter Eyes,
           I
           choose
           you.

And I pray that our
Pilgrimage
around
the
North Star
does not end

Until **Blackness** is
infinite,

infinitely.

Papyrus:
Because Your Watercolors Move Me

A type of lyrical constipation,
I am searching for the words to portray an image
that has no physical equivalent;
I am searching for the words to provide a proper context,
to accurately portray erroneous emotion,
a feeling that is pure,
        but untimely....

I'm not quite sure who
      you
        are,
            but every time I look at you,
              I wonder what you look
        like in *words*.
        And it seems that when you stare
        at me,
            You are patiently
            converting me to an
            acrylic image.

And sometimes I even wonder if you take me home
And   **g** me on your wall,
   n
h **a**
Or if the portrait that you've painted
Dissipates by day-clean.

How do I paint mystery with *words*?

How do I depict PASSION
        on **paper?**

What type of ancient code or *script* must I study
To find ONE
      word that captures you?

Should I revert to hieroglyphics,

Cuneiform characters?

Perhaps the word is B
                      U
                      R
                                    IED layers deep
On a random piece of papyrus.
Wherever it be,
  I may have to cross
                          land and sea
                    to find it
'Cause *love* is the easy way out…
This ain't love.
This is Righteous and delicious.
This is freedom and captivity.
This…has kept me up all night!

      And I simply can't sleep until I've painted you with
      my words.

Meanwhile, far off in the d i s t a nce
                    of my one track mind,
I'm curious whether your watercolors
Are still comfortably tucked away in their storage place.
            Have I inspired you to *lift* a brush? -
            Enough just to see whether watercolors
            will do,
            Or if only *acrylic* does my beauty justice?

'Cause I have not peacefully rested in d a y s

In search of the proper words to paint you.

And perhaps you do not know the reason
For the bags under my eyes,
But indeed they carry the weight of words that
Sound
  impressive
and
  mean
    nothing,
And I pray that you see past them
To a **GLOW** that you've inspired…

A light that *can't* be photographed...
A light that *must* be painted.
And the bags under my eyes
Will be **weighted** with words
H
 e
a
  vy
and
   HOLLOW

Until you are as beautiful
     on paper
     as you are
     in person.

And whatever words I find to capture you,
I pray they be in FUTURE tense.

And somewhere in my daydreams
There is a *Divine* depiction of me
    g
   n
  i
   g
    n
   a
  h
proudly on your wall of thoughts.

Excavated Treasures

It's funny, the difference a day makes...
And the difference the Hand of God makes
in matters of the Heart.
So we celebrate the opportunity to
                                  f
                                         a
                                         |
                                   |
                            into submission -
                            this time consciously,
                      For the lighthouse of the
             Spirit also functions as a *storehouse-*

      when we listen.

        Respect.
        Only love and *respect...*

                Is it *antiquated*?

                        Is my language a bit *cryptic?*

                Is my character *archaic?*

                    Could it be that my spirit was
                    excavated
                    alongside *dinosaur bones?*

And could *that* be the very spot God
            mo l ded and blew breath
            into yours?

Am I brave enough to dig where
        "X" marks the spot?

Or shall I find myself waiting for the surface to e r o De
                                                            from
                                                              weathering...

I am reminded that "faith is the evidence of things unseen."

Treasures lie buried deep,
and good things come to THOSE
                                WHO
                                  WAIT,
but *better* things come to those
                                who follow the instruction
                                of the Most High within.

And I shudder to think of consequences!

Because how often do we meet at the apex of the TRI-angle
                              in a beautiful TRInity?

How often do we witness *Providence?*

So here I stand,
                        And *HERE* I dig

                                      to excavate my treasures.

I Call You Zen

I call you ZEN in the meantime
Because peace is the fruit of the spirit
That is not forbidden, but rather rare…
A dear to spring water,
You are walking FENG SHUI,
        a moving meditation.
Sunrays peeking through forest canopies,
So I call you ZEN.

You are April pollen and May sap,
Evening fires and overnight ashes tempting the stratosphere.
A **BEAM** of Gamma rays,
Light traveling at
                the
                speed
                of
                sound,

'Cause ain't no
            need to rush a
                        thang…

You –
    are moments *s a v o r e d.*
Footsteps after morning
                r
                a
                i
                n
                s,
A waterfall with belly **full**
        boasting Tropical Skittles.
Snow-capped mountains worthy of
                postcard portraiting;

I call you ZEN.

Wind and thistles,
Flowering Dogwood...
Yeshua smiles.
The Gardenias and Impatiens
   have never been so fulfilled –

Your ZEN is water and solar energy,
   A channel of Truth,
   A vortex of
   violet light
   and
   velvet
   visions.

You are Sunstone and Green Tourmaline.
You are yellow manifested,
   Love on *legs*.
      You are ZEN.

While you were sleeping,
The day was dreaming of *you*,
Waiting to be greeted,
   B
   A
   S
   K
   in your cool.

I call you Abishalom –
   father of peace.
Alafia knows you by name.
Your features are reminiscent
   of Tutankhamen,
And your Spirit is *draped in white*;
   Gold and brass would appreciate you.
Rock gardens,
   crystal oceans,
   ...Inspired stalks of bamboo.

Bonsai trees b
        o
          w,

Stream waters form ripples in the tide,
And sHaDeS of
      Brown,
        Black,
          and
      Purple are **DEIFIED**.
I need you...

And you love me not because of what I *do*,
But simply because I am
      nothing
      in particular.
I call you ZEN in the meantime -
A walking FENG SHUI,

    a moving meditation...

I call you...
    Revolution.

Marco Polo

I've been r u n n ing from my words,
but desperate traces of their shadows
haunt my night dreams
and permeate vivid day dreams
seeking to shatter the outer shells
       of my independent thinking -
Relentlessly aiming to prove that I do,
                        in fact,
            feel the way
                I
               say
                I
               don't.

I'm runnin' fast...
but the Truth is on my heels
and it's gainin' on me,
and my heart's beating *twice* as fast
because I'm only *half* its size.

       And you know what?

I think I'll even stop chastising the
clumsy white girl in the horror films
'Cause we always talk about what we would do
when the monster's on *OUR* tails...
thinkin' we're Billy Bad-Ass,
but we're still lowercase g's.
No, I'm not turnin' around and looking that
       Monster
         in
          the
           face -
What the hell would I say?

       I'm not brave enough to be loved...

...I'm runnin' FAST! GALE DEVERS
...no, no, think JACKIE JOYNER!

No, no, think white folks when
Blacks and Mexicans start
movin' in...
I'M GETTIN' THE HELL ON!

    I don't know how to be loved just because...

Damn that! I'm Usain Bolt out this joint!

    Because I know that I could love you past November
        into eternity
    until we've *become* rice and sweet berries
    for our Great-Great Grandchildren to eat.
    See, I know that I could love you *past* your
        past lives....

Don't you know ***my love*** is the reason the dinosaurs didn't make it??
    Natural selection...
    only the strongest survive –
        Right?

So you can call me Hurricane Andrew,
And I'll be damned if you catch me -

    'Cause I don't feel like finding out if what I think
    about you is true.

And I don't care if you're the matchless love I've
prayed for though the ages!
And I could give a rat's ass if we used to be
neighboring stars
or our souls have been linked since we traveled down
together on a chain from Heaven with the OrISHa -
So *what* loving you would be as sacred as the
Arc of the Covenant?!

I'm good by my *damn* self,
because then I could rest assured that
I'll always have loving arms to cradle me...

Even if they're my own.

What do you mean I sound SCARED?!
I'm not scared, I'm just —

    Cautious.

Because we don't always get out what we put in,

    And I know that I love hard...

    I can already feel the discrepancy between my words and my actions:

    I'm calling you five times a day just to tell you how much I **don't** care,
    Tryin' not to sound too *invested* in your
        well-being.
    Entertaining my emotional discourse
        FOR PAGES UPON PAGES
    to say that you are **not** worth my time,
        nor my words,
    nor the ink that bleeds my DNA onto this paper,
    in hopes that you can't see through this
        silly
            ass
        front
    that I recognized some time ago
    as a poor defense mechanism.

I've got good reason for runnin' from my words...

    'CAUSE STANZAS EXPRESSING
UNPRECEDENTED PASSION
        HAVE BEEN **beating**   **breaks**
                the   **off**
                        my
                            brain,

AND I CAN ONLY IMAGINE WHAT THEY'D DO
    to paper.
And worse, imagine what my mind is doin' to you when you're
      not   looking.

    Thinking of you is sensory overload
    Because for some reason the synaptic **g a p**
    between imagination and physical stimulus
    gets much smaller when it comes to you.

    And I spend my days wondering what your
    neurotransmitters are thinking of me.

    And whether my voice inspires them to **fire** the way
                              yours
                              does.
    And what if it doesn't?

    ...But what if it does?
        And you meet me at the vortex of our
        sacred Trinity,
        and you bring God **with** you?

    And we heal the hearts of nations with one pen.

"Marco!"
        "Polo!"

...IF YOU CAN CATCH ME,

    you can keep me,

            Forever.

Pretty pictures

Paint me a **pretty picture**
to inspire my Spirit
To soar through constellations unseen with the naked eye.

Inspire me to love harder, breathe easier, see **clearer**.
Inspire me to remember...
That I *can* be as free as DANDELIONS IN THE WIND.
Hungry Spirits grow thirsty
when appetites are not fulfilled.

So, my confidant,
    inspire me
       to be unabashed,
       and vehemently pursue new beginnings.

Inspire me to lead and be Led to unchartered territory.
Inspire my Spirit to be daring,
    and unapologetic.
Inspire me to break through the mold not yet formed,
To *set* the precedent,
To leave
    Heavy Footprints on the Path
    Designed for me.

And, be reminded,
Kindred Spirit,
You have not
    forgotten
    how
      to love.

Let the watercolors
    within you   **oils on**
      emerge like   **the**
                    page.

You are ready.
Do not allow *Principalities* to convince you
that your worries carry more weight
than a single
  b   r   u   s   h - stroke
across empty space…

Husband, you are mighty…
Paint pretty pictures to remind you,
And you'll remember how to love.
Allow the pastels *within* you to encourage my sensibilities,
     And love me
back
     to life time
         and time again…

I Just Want You to Know:
A Tangential Romantic Epithet

He says I'm the Sunshine in his pocket,
But little does he know
that he's my Light at the end of the Tunnel,

My blessed indication that I did it right,

My physical sign that my destiny's been anointed,

My not-so-subtle reminder that it wasn't all for nothing,

A way to know that Spirit is signing off on my progress report,

A PIECE OF GOD'S SMILE TO CARRY IN MY PURSE ·

Break me off a piece like **Kit Kat**, and savor it S.L.O.W.L.Y.

You get me to thinkin' that forever ain't so long,
And sometimes I find myself askin' God for an extension,
Cause forever might end *too soon*.

So I gotta **WRITE**,
RIGHT
RIGHT NOW,
To record this moment in time that shall pass and return in my memory.

Is it tangential, per se?
Um, more like isosceles...

But I just wanted to remind you that you're appreciated.

And you look just like that piece of God I saw in the flowering dogwood tree,
And the running brook that I sat at to pray the other day.
You look *just* like that.

Phyl•liz Sóph°i˙kăl
the Phonetician

And sometimes I get intimidated to look directly
into your eyes for extended periods,
Cause only the brave surrender to *Rapture*.

      Well, **AM I BRAVE??**

I just might be, but the one time I tried
I was tempted to re-enact a scene from *Jason's Lyric*
with you....

(dramatic pause)

Yeah, the one where they were sitting on the bridge,
And he turned and said,
      "I AINT NEVA SEEN THE SUN SET BEFO'."

                        Sh*t, me neither.
                        I mean, not like this.

But it's just like that, I mean, you're *just* like that.
No, no, not like the sunset.
You're *just* like that...
      that bridge on which they sat.
Kinda puts me in the mind of Westminster Abbey,
And the Romantic and Transcendental Poetry
      I became enamored with in Eleventh Grade.

And I just want you to know...
I just want you to know...

And I *can't* tell you.
And this telepathy thing doesn't work like it used to
Cause there's too much to distract us in the modern age.
So I just draw pictures in the sand,
And hope that the message hits home
And resonates somewhere in your subconscious.
Yeah, I appreciate you.

      And it looks a lot like *lollipops and swords*,
                            ya know?

The sweet and the *oh so very* dangerous…

And it's a good thing you remind me of a bridge
And not my Jeep,
'Cause I sooooo could…but I won't,
'Cause it's not time yet.
But I just want you to know…

And I want you to look me in my eyes,
And tell me that you understand
Without saying a word at all.
But I mean, I honor your creativity,
And of course there are OTHER ways to go about it,
And that's cool too.

**But I just want you to know….
I just want you to know.**

So show me that my pictures in the sand were effective,
Give me a sign that will breech the divide
    Like a flare gun, or, cannonballs,
    Or send me a note upstream,
    And I respond to you by Dove,
And perhaps I'll enclose some mistletoe…

And then we can dream,
 if we're lucky,
  in COLOR.
And I promise I'll remember how many petals were on the flower
As I sat counting by

  LOVE
   ME'S
  aNd
  LOVE
   ME
  NOTS.

I promise to stay fixated on the Light at the End of the Tunnel,
And I can only pray that if I am to be the Sunshine in your pocket,
        That I do it *right*.

Cause I'm scared,
and I carry bravery on my shoulders -
        But not on my chest like armor.

And I hope you can find it in your heart to forgive me
For sometimes feeling tempted to go into battle
        without my breastplate -
It's in the mail.

And I just want you to know...
I just want you to know.

Please just send me a message that you understand,
And if I can block out the radio and *CELL*   T
                                      PHONE   O
                                                          W
                                                          E
                                                          R
                                                          S

                                        in my mind...

    I will get it.

    And I will know too.

aSankofaTypaLuv

Your
love
is
ancient,
      and noble.
I'm hopeful, so hopeful-
I'm hopeful that when S   M
                            U   O
                            N & O
                            S   N
                                    S
                                  align

Your energy Divine
will intertwine with mine
And we'll sip fine wine,
Feast and dine on perfect portions.
                True love
                bears no distortions,
We lie in oceans,
bathe in its motions.
                Ebb and flow like emotions
                and uncommitted devotion.

Your eyes remind me of that time centuries ago
When you rocked your locks,
And I rocked my fro.
We danced for the rain to come,
And prayed for the wind to b l o w.
We were connected with Spirit and Earth,
      And now,
           we celebrate rebirth…
Because, see, that was back then,
That was back when
Time was of the essence, yet of no consequence.
And now we've been reborn. But we remember the corn…

Paradise.   Shea Trees.   Righteous energies.
-

The **b r e e z e.**
       Do you believe?
       Can we go back there?
       Is it wrong to long for love that
                  transcends the ages?
One that goes beyond the binding and beyond the pages,
    beyond the words to their essence and meaning…
        Dawn 'til dusk and morn 'til evening
                You'll find me dreaming
Of love made Supremely, between Supreme Beings.
        See, I want to feel that time in X-Y-Z   B.C.
        When you picked passionfruit for me,
            And we feasted floating in the sea,
            And we could simply be.
               So do you believe?
                 In Powers and Principalities?
                   Multiplicitous Deities?
                     Oneness?
                     Me?
                     Intimacy?
                     Being free?
    Could it be that time capsules really *do* exist?
        Then, we fought for Our tribe,
        And today we raise Our fist.
Then I carried the river water upon a steady head –
The Sun was my pillow, and the Moon was my bed.
      You were *Elegba*, in your black and red…
      I was *Oshun*, and we were wed.
      You washed my feet with berry juice
            And
          We loved
            Hard.
       We've come so far,
       and Africa's
        Still
       In our backyard.
    …a Sankofa Typa Love.

Oracle and Warrior
(aSankofaTypaLuv, Part II)

◊Eden was so beautiful,
Well, it was *Nubia* then.
We loved hard.
We grew old.
We passed on.
And they remembered us in prayer...

We emerged from humble beginnings -
As *oracle* and *warrior*,
We complimented each other's righteousness
Because I *knew*, and you *fought*,
And we blew the breath of Life into
        twelve Tribes...

◊I returned,
the victim of a stolen legacy –
They snatched me from the Shea Tree,

    Took the baby.
                    BRANDED MY BROTHER,

Muttered something about *Christianity*-
                          I SHUDDERED.

I searched for you amidst the **CHAOS**,
Carried you in my Spirit as they forced me upon the ship,
Dreamed about our baby
That they snatch
        ed from my hip.
I grit my teeth,
bit my lip until it bled,
Shuffled in the shackles
and out of shame,

DIDACTIC DOPAMINE

L
  o
    w
      e
        r
          e
            d
my
head.

They sat me down,
And I lifted my eyes in surprise -
You SURVIVED...
And it looked as though you'd been waiting;
I'd hoped to find you, but not like this.
      We endured the voyage –
         Clenched teeth, tight fists, we grueled,
      And all we had was each other...
But I *knew*, and you *fought*,
         So we broke free-
           Stood on the deck, jumped into the sea,
             Confident that in the next lifetime,
             You'd find ME.

◊I was born to Mary and Jessie in 1837 –
I was one of eleven when Daddy got sold,
The day I turned fifteen years old.
I cried, but momma told me one day we'd be
    free...
I remembered freedom –
The day before the Shea tree,
But that was *centuries* ago and
My prayers are the only freedom I know.
I prayed for you, prayed for your safety;
And I knew God was good the day you came to me –
        Sold off the Adams Plantation onto mine.
        I recognized you... you
             were
             stoic,
             Black,
             and fine;
        Our love had endured over three lifetimes.

But I *knew*, and you *fought*,
>> So one night you took to runnin'
>> **And I ran *with* you.**
>> We found freedom through underground channels.
>> We grew old, and our lives were recorded in the annals…

◊I returned in 1920, marched with Garvey;
>> I looked good in Red, Black and Green,

You thought so, too, when we met in '33 –
You approached me with familiarity,
You remembered my smile…
you couldn't forget me.
>> You were in the army, got a letter in '43.
>>> I stood at the port,
>>> Waved a damp, white
>>>> handkerchief in your support.
>> You wrote me in '44,
>> and I felt your spirit dwindling,

Cause I *knew*, and you *fought*…
>> My worst fears were confirmed, but I was determined to find you –

>> **It was a game of tag,**
>> **And I was *IT*…**

◊My mother waited 'til she was thirty to have me –
I almost thought I wouldn't make it.

>> My search for you began immediately…

In the meantime, I reveled in the arts –
>> *Music, dance, poetry.*
>> I liked Hip-Hop, but I loved **NINA SIMONE,**
>> I couldn't wait to find you 'cause I hated being alone.
I was confident that you were waiting to be tagged,
>> **'Cause history repeats itself…**
>> Five centuries later
>> and I *still* couldn't help myself.

I *still* carried you in my spirit,
I still *knew,* and you *fought...*

I thought I peeped you one day on Auburn Ave.,
    Then again in the Fall on Old National,
Thought it might've been you with the Fatherhood T-Shirt on the yard,
    Finally, I realized I was lookin' too hard.
Fooled myself into thinking that I'd let **you find me,**
    But I only found myself searching
        more aggressively.
    Thought I'd sight you at one of my readings,
    Or perhaps at one of yours –
    You always did appreciate the power of the spoken word.
Was that you at the Roots concert?
        Naw...that was just my homie Bird.

...One night, I prayed real hard,
And asked God to send you to me from wherever you were...

Days Pass...

So I was **CHILLIN',**
    ENJOYIN'
      THE
      HELL
        OUTTA
    SOME
      JERK CHICKEN,
    Engaging in some quality stomach rubbin' and finger licking...
There was a disturbance outside,
sirens all around,
I saw five cops knock this brotha to the ground.

It was real foggy out,
but I could clearly see through the mist

The **permanently engraved**

>MARKS
>ON
>HIS WRIST.

I asked if he'd been arrested before,
He said "NO",
    and I thought,
        "BULLSH*T."

…Three months later, I served on a jury and
    he was the accused,
He was innocent…
    don't ask me how I *knew*.
But all odds were against him,
    and I knew that he would lose.
They sentenced him to life,
And it just didn't sit right on my conscience;
He kept looking at me as though **pleading** for my help;
I thought about the

>MARKS
>ON
>HIS WRIST

    and couldn't help myself,
      'Cause they looked a lot like mine…

That's when it clicked…

I *knew*, and you *fought*,
    But they made the verdict stick.

> **…I see you on Sundays,**
> **and between time I write,**
> **Just to die to be re-born.**

        So we can get it right.

EPISODE 2:

"LOST GENERATION FAST-PACED NATION WORLD POPULATION CONFRONT THEY FRUSTRATION..."

-*Never Do (What They Do)*, The Roots (1996)

Enter-mission

Deepest Secrets hidden,
Thoughts written under ~~scratches~~ and SCRIBBLES.
Feel my **FRUSTRATION**,
    my **pseudo-elation**,
Precipitated results of my

        alienation.

The ceaseless teasing and taunting,
Ridicule haunting
      my mind,
Exhaustion WARPING my paradigm.

Tired of playing the "*Strong Black Woman*"
All the damn time!

Fighting to release the demons of the past –
Things that remain

    ...UNADDRESSED.

Meanwhile, I wear the MASK -

They say I wear it *well*...

Stripper Culture
(Dancin' for Dingy Dollaz)

I spend my days at Club Nicki's and my nights at Jazzy T's,
Dancin' for dirty dollars while I'm ~~scuffy~~' up my knees,
Takin' off my clothes on stage with these other
~~hoes~~

While these HALIBURTONS are callin' us
SAMBOS.

We're pros at compromising from our titties to our toes
Dressed in
the
     business
suits
 that we bought in THEIR stores

With THEIR dirty money
that we earned by bein'
~~hoes~~.

And they told us to bend over and touch 'em…

And we do it.

And our mental's sayin' **"F*CK 'EM!"**…

     And we *do* it -

Or should I say they f*ck us…
Stuffin' single dollars down our draws

To feed our babies.

And We keep on strippin' cause we're figurin' just *maybe*
When all this shit is over,
we can live like them…
'House on the hill with the white picket fence.'

They holla, "Take it off,"

    So we give them integrity.

They holla, "Take it off,"

    We compromise serenity.

They holla, "Where da Hooooes at?"

    And I quickly answer,

"Me."
They said,
"Take the scarf off. We don't care about your
allah!
If you keep it on, you won't get paid

And so I took it
        off.

DIDACTIC DOPAMINE

Takin' off my clothes for dollars
Then holla I'm a 'scholar on *Afrocentricity*,'
Yet I relinquished the freedom
that Harriet helped give to me.
Dancin' for dollars,
whatever dance they wanna see…
    FILE THESE PAPERS,
                ANSWER THE PHONE,

        SUCK MY D*CK FOR ME.
It's all the same…
and we *do* it.
Strippin' for dingy dollars,
Removing our self-worth,
      our ***culture***,
             our *religion*,
and SMILE like it doesn't hurt.
Gave up my native tongue
 and
the covering on my head,
I let them take me,
rape me,
and then leave me for
dead…

…"Look ma, I found a dollar. It was stuck down in my draws!…
And with it I found
pink private parts broke off between my walls.

He told me be to work at five, and so I've gotta go
Finish *dancin'* for my dollars…

    I'm the feature in the show."

Institutional Prostitution
(Reflections of a Strange Bed-Fellow)

My COUNTRY tis of thee
And I think they said sweet dreams are made of these too,
These fantasies that they call liberties,
That they're supposedly granting me,
But I know it's blasphemy.
See, time keeps passin' me
And as time proceeds I feel more and more like a strange bed-fellow –
She keeps touchin' me, tryin' to brush up to me
But suspicions keep rushin' me.

She keeps tellin' me how Great I am,
How proud to be an AMERICAN,
But she keeps goin' through my grits,
And I'm sick and tired of it!
And I feel like Chuckii Booker,
"Why you wanna try and play your games on me?!"
She be stalkin' me when I don't want her nowhere 'round,
But when I really *need* her, chick ain't nowhere to be found,
And they call these fantasies
     LIBERTIES!
I call it trickery!
INSTITUTIONAL PROSTITUTION ...

She stays sexin' my body and rapin' my soul
And the madness gets old.

So I keeps my calcium on deck
so
I
can
strengthen
my
bones
and stand for something this country told me was wrong...

Indeed, I am "**black and comely!**"

And quite endowed with intelligence,
Tryin' to speak Truth to power
'Cause they've been counting on our ignorance
Ever since the nose got **SHOT OFF** the Sphinx,
And nobody wants to admit to stickin' their hand in the cookie jar...

They tried to blame it on weatherin',
Just like they tried to blame the
weather when
         the levees **BROKE.**
Tell the truth about the arms
 you used to bomb them
In order to displace a population throughout the nation!
I will not be deceived...

...Unless of course you pull a trick out your sleeve
That we have never seen before,
Like *actually* letting the first
Black
        PRESIDENT

      live
without sabotaging his career,
Diggin' up some old dirt,
 or hiring your
   MILITIA,
And when they get caught,
calling them
      everyday civilians.
I will not be surprised,
Nor sit idly by while the boy who cried wolf
Pulls the wool
over our eyes!

I STAY WOKE.

Pipe Dreams: When Chicken Noodle Soup is not Enough

They told me all I need is **chicken soup** to heal my soul
So I stuffed in my heart as many dreams as it would hold.
    I tried chicken soup, lemon juice, honey, green tea,
    And still my past would not let me be free,
    So I let it be -
Took faith into my own hands and devised a remedy.
    And here I stand, hand FULL OF PIPES
    And a belly **FULL OF ROCKS**,
    The stench of it lingering faintly in my locks.
I'm caught up ya'll.

I'm a **serpent crying tears**
For all the **pain** that I've felt over the years.
Can't face my fears 'cause
the gears keep shifting on me
Reflection in the mirrors force me to see I'm lonely.
Too much stress for one man to face alone,

So it was **SQUARES** to grass and grass to **STONES**

Took so much of my body, I can't call it my own,
Damaged my temple and ~~destroyed~~ my home.
They judge me and don't even *bother* to ask why
I had to turn to this poison,
'Cause if they did then I'd reply that

I'm a Black woman, victim of **rape** and assault,
At the age of eight I
became an
>   A
>   D
>   U
>   L
>   t,

At the age of nine, I'd say I was fine,
Find the neighborhood dope-man and cop me a
dime.
By the age of ten, I was swimmin' in sin,
No need to defend my innocence 'cause it was gone
by then.
At the age of eleven I had dreams about *Heaven*,
But
left those dreams
>   to
>   be
>   dream'd
>   by that girl that was seven

That didn't know her childhood would end so soon,
    Muffling my screams
            while Mom was in the next room
            For twenty-nine suns and
            thirty moons.

You do the math.

At the age of twelve, I looked out for self,
While nicks and dimes controlled my health.
At age thirteen was declared a feign,

DIDACTIC DOPAMINE

Had known more **strife** than some
    A
    D
    U
    L
    t
    S had seen.
I remember a court scene at age fourteen -
Somethin' about intention to distribute weed.
Roamed halls with numbers across my chest,
And what seemed to be lasers
                        pointed at my head.
I predicted by sixteen I would be ~~dead~~.
I stood corrected
'cause seventeen rolled around

And now I was out, in alleys trickin' for pounds.

At eighteen, from what I'd known I was considered grown,
But in my heart, in my mind,
It had been a long, long time since I was
       child.
          Wild, beautiful, and
          free as the *Nile*.
At nineteen I was on corners with boots
too high to walk in,
Skirts showin' my fruits,
Doing what I had never dreamed in my youth.
You know, the one that was stolen-
Permanent damage to my rectum and colon.
The one that had induced so much pain that I
tucked it away beneath a flame
And *puuuuulled* until I had no name, no face,

and nothing else my mattered
But a cloud.
Of these things I am not proud,
But if you listen closely,
you'll hear

a
   cry
     so loud

Because deep within me there still exists a
    Child,
So flighty and free as a floater -
If you looked a bit closer…

I think you'd know her.

Calamine Lotion
(Mama the Bumps Don't Itch No Mo')

Half man, half martian, eh?
Water baby and star child...
Perhaps we were neighboring stars after all -

CLIP! Red wire!

Pressurized passion **e x p l o des** matter into space like shrapnel,
No more runnin'.
Dandelions have suffered stampedes long enough.
Stop, and admire its
      medicinal value!
Too many dandelions die under the feet of
fearful men:

Are we brave enough to be the
      substitute for penicillin?

      Healing words like calamine lotion -
"Mama, the bumps don't itch no mo'!"

...Baby takes the **RED PILL** and lays back down

to awaken to a world he doesn't quite understand.
It's an army out there, and
pr i nci pal i t i es
enter combat with weapons unfamiliar to mere men.

Put your guns away,
your M-16's are no good here.
REAL NIGGAZ don't bring guns
to a battle over *principalities*;
We fight with words and
>balanced chakras
>>out here playa...

>Healing words like calamine lotion,
"Mama, the bumps don't itch no mo'!"

"Baby, lay back down,
Mama's gotta go be the syringe to dis-eased existences.

Insert me directly into the bloodstream
and watch **O negative** become **B**(e) **positive**;

YOUR BLOODTYPE IS **GOD** AND DON'T
LET THEM TELL YOU OTHERWISE!"

We are children of the elements,
and the struggle towards a Dignity that they recognize
necessarily involves the invocation of your
>ELEMENTAL FORCES:

fire baby.
Form your comets and *toss* them like canons -
FIGHT!

Earth baby.
Sprinkle broken shards of amethyst into the soil,
Regrow our crystal **FORTRESSES**

Phyl■liz Sóph°i˘kăl
the Phonetician

that interrupt the skies -
FIGHT!

Child of the strong winds:
Invoke your wind-storm essence,
Feet circle *feverishly*,
YOU are the tornado personified -
FIGHT!

Water baby,
Birth nations, nurture and nestle
OMNIPOTENCE,
Negate iniquity,
And never break your ankles on the shoreline as you ebb and flow -
But FIGHT!

I'm done running,
I'm offering myself as a living sacrifice,
A testimony to the power of a mission accepted;
Committed to being your syringe,
A proper substitute for Penicillin...

        Healing words like calamine lotion,
"Mama, the bumps don't itch no mo'!"

...Baby takes the **RED PILL** and lays back down.

He awakens to find wires loosened from his cerebral cortex -
He's unplugged,
      but he ain't scared...

Baby was nurtured and nestled into the infantry commissioned to rebuild our crystal fortresses with our **WORDS** –

        Healing words like calamine lotion,
    "Mama, the bumps don't itch no mo'!"

Baby can't lay back down.

SOLDIERS
DON'T SLEEP
WHERE
THERE
IS
WAR.

Letter from a Concerned "Citizen"

**"Black bodies hangin' in the southern breeze,
Strange fruit hangin' from the poplar trees..."**
  -*Strange Fruit*, Billie Holiday
   (Adopted by Nina Simone)

I wonder if they'll be honest with you
about the poplar trees,
And why she never got that Grammy she so well deserved.
I suppose they expected her satisfaction with the
15 nominations...
I, FOR ONE, AM NOT.
And not because she didn't win an award
that was created by their standards,
But because they
          still
won't tell the truth about the poplar trees...
And why is it that I'm looked at sideways
When I proclaim to have heard them
screaming "JUSTICE" to me too?

"Blood at the roots and blood on the leaves..."
Well, there's **life** in the blood,
So, Yes! I heard them!
And Yes! They sang woeful melodies
synchronized with the swaying of branches
In unapologetic winds.

But let it be known that strange fruit don't just
grow in the South,
It's just that in the South
                      it's a *ca$h crop* -
And they won't be honest with you.
So tell me **MR. PRESIDENT**,
Why won't you be honest
with the people you claim to represent,
And hold true to the ideals you never upheld.
Tell them about the poplar trees!
Tell them how you stood there with your rifles and
your children,
And SMILED.
And took pictures by his foot that **D**
                                           A
                                           N
                                           G
                                           L
                                           E
                                         D lifeless –

Tell them about your madness!
About how it was recorded in your
genetic and ontological memory,
So that their children never witnessed it **firsthand**,
but love the smell of urine and fresh blood.

Got dammit tell them the truth about the poplar trees!

Tell them about the legacy we inherited,
And don't you dare pretend not to know!
Tell them about the ways you
strategically tried to hide it,

And reinforce the lies through institutions.
Tell them why more children have been left behind since
It was said that "No child [would be] left behind"!
Go ahead and tell them!
Tell them that you *wanted* them left behind,
And if it wasn't for the exploitation
of cheap but well-skilled labor,
You *would have* left them where they were
in their **BUSHES AND LOINCLOTHS**...
Until of course you decided to civilize and develop them into the

Third World Nations
        you *still* refer to them as.
Tell them that Don Imus
and Bill O'Reilly
and
our beloved Kramer from Seinfeld
Meant what they said…
Their **APOLOGIES** don't mean $h%t!

Come on, Mr. President,
You like to make public addresses
And speeches that other people write for you,
So here's your script…

"Here's THE TRUTH about the poplar trees…"

Tell them what you really wanted to achieve in Iraq.
Tell them that you don't like
    your *own* niggers,
And you don't like sand niggers, either.

This is what you've told your children,
And your children have said it to me,
So won't you just admit that's how you feel!
Won't you tell your children that they are entitled
to exercise their
privilege
Because they are reflections of a
Great Race,
But won't you tell them that you don't even like
    yourself,
And you can't stand the idea of a people
who have so much power and integrity
that you wanted to strip it away,

      by
Layer   *layer,*

Century by century –

Won't you tell them why nose on the **SPHINX** is missing!

Tell them the Truth about the poplar trees!

Tell them why you sometimes have **dreams** about
    them,
And in the quietest hour,
when no one is looking,
You wish they could replace the electric chair,
So you could invite your family, friends,
And the **WHOLE DAMN NEIGHBORHOOD**
to witness an angel's fate.

The blood is
in
the
roots,

The life is
in
the
blood,

And the legacy
is
in
the
song.

Ms. Simone, it's about time you got your Grammy...

Left to Write

They rule and control me,
Hold me close to their objectives,
peel and **penetrate** my purpose,
Circumcise my cool and calm
mannerisms.
FORCE me to my apex   ,
Vexed, volatile, and vindictive
destinations.
Stressed vocal chords don't seem like *peace*,
So if sToCCaTo inflections and volumes
decrease,
MAYBE WE'LL *GET* SOMEWHERE IN THIS MUTHA –

………

Please forgive my momentary deviation from my mature and appropriate approach…

Agreements to be civil
contain me in my cage,
Never to engage in results of
        secret rage.
I rediscover my peace within this page,
And reach lower numbers in degrees Fahrenheit,
Vexation vanishes
as my hand goes left
                to write.

Reflections on Lyrical Alchemy
(For Hip-Hop Headz Everywhere)

Best believe that everything I ~~touch~~ turns to gold.

You won't hear me talkin' 'bout bustin' and 44's,
I'm tryin' to keep it Righteous…
I don't even *own* those.
Won't catch me sellin' my soul/spittin' 'bout takin' off my clothes
Or freaky acts that go on behind closed doors.
My mind's eye is PLATINUM,
And I won't sell out for radios.
It ain't my role to talk about poppin' twats and touchin' toes -
I can't settle for silver

When everything I touch is gold.

Consumers support the lies,
but I'ma give you the facts:
Once you speak words,
    YOU
    CAN
    NEVER
    GET
    THEM
BACK,
So, it's about time we gave a damn about
What we put on wax.
'Cause everything that you speak is recorded in time
Every *word*, every *syllable*, every *letter*
    and *rhyme*.

But it seems though,
That cats don't care **NoMMo**
about ⓦⓞⓡⓓ
Sound
POWER.
No concern for the hour that we expire.
No longer able to fix our lips
To R̶E̶M̶I̶X̶
   the chicks
       F#cked,
               D*cks sucked,
      Guns
         Bust…
No more opportunities to fix
Us.
To re-write,
~~un-write~~
the words that were spoken –
What about Higher Powers revokin'
Your last chance to say that you were
      'jokin'.
The game is slowly changing
Is what I'm hopin' –
Or maybe wishfully thinkin' –
I'm just doing my part to keep cats
double   **BLINKIN'**.
'Cause I'm just GUTTA enough
to ensure that people listen
But just _{subtle} enough
To make sure that you ain't missin'
The <u>bottom lines</u> of my **punch lines**…

DIDACTIC DOPAMINE

I *been* preachin' that we keep teachin',
Be brave enough to remove the leaches
From our mind's eye –
I…
I…simply cannot stand by
While these cats keep spittin' ignorance
They're mad at me 'cause my **POETICS**
have been hurtin' feelings since
Nineteen eighty-six.

Who said you can't be lyrical
With a nice flow
Without callin' me a **hoe**
Or a *B*tch*?
Who said you can't be sick with it,
Make people feel it,
Be quick-witted
And still get it
Like LUCKY LUCIANO
or some paid Italiano?

I'ma get that bread
Fo sho',
But one thing you gotta know:

I WON'T SELL OUT FOR RADIO…

And if I gotta be whack to be in the mainstream
Then I don't want it,
And if I can't be Black and still do my thing,
Then I won't front. If
I gotta be naked to work the scene,
Then I won't flaunt it,
'Cause I do have the mind of a Queen

And the heart of a
Servant.

And I'm not sayin' that my slate is clean
And my life is perfect,
But I know what the *purpose*
Of my Presence on
Earth is.

I am an artist, a lyricist -
And I pray I've *touched* your soul.

I may not make it on radio,
But everything I *touch*

is góld.

She Was God:
An Ode to Hip-Hop

I spent twenty-two years searching for *God*,
Looking for her among Cumulus and Cirrus clouds,
Searching for her in some ambiguous layer between
the blues of Heaven
        and the **BLACKS** of Space.
Just to realize that to limit God to these domains
Traps her in a box to circumnavigate
like mimes.
And though I found evidence of Her dwelling there,
I too found traces of her footsteps on Earth...

She rocked **Nike Airs**...and a thick, gold rope chain
With a fuzzy KANGOL cocked to the side, grill GLEAMIN'.

And she moved me...

She moved me like Earth's simultaneous motions around the sun.

She moved me like baby's hand on **hot stove**,
Like Bare Feet on hot concrete,
Like the devastation of `crack cocaine`...

I was *moved.*

And she was not esoteric.
I understood her
because she was familiar.
I knew her like I know that
one plus two is *three-sixty*.
And indeed she was Divine.
She was Spiritual Transformation,
    emotional confusion,
  Rapture,
the Beginning,
    the **END**,
  and
  the beginning again -
She was *God*.
And I ran toward her light.
She did not deny me, shun me,
or damn me to infernal eternities.
She welcomed me with open arms
      draped in BaNGLeS,
and I rested my head FIRMLY on her
    bamboo doorknockers,
  and I knew that she was REAL.

She was the RENEX personified, she was NOMMO,

She WAS the *Living Word*.

And she said, "Let there be Light,"
and there was, and she saw that it was good.
And she said, "Let there be dark,"
and there was, and she saw that it was good.
And she said, "Let there be
Chicano,
Latino,

Asian, Rasta,
    Native American,
Pacific Islander,
    Trini,
Amerindian,
    Zulu,
European,
    Korean,
Central American,
    Canadian,
and Kenyan,

and let them all move under the command of my

V()ICE· · ·

And they did.

And she saw that it was good...It was real good.

Mattafact, it was **ALL good**.

And she commanded that the masses unite
in the name of something far greater than
themselves.
She commanded that they move to a harmonious
sTaccaTo,
So one
upon another,
and to the next,
they moved.

And the energy welled up
from **STURDY** ankles,
to desperate knees,
to tempted hips,
to arching backs,
to BOBBIN' necks,
to two **enchanted** fingers extended into a
⊑⊔⊏⊀⊐⊢⊡⊤.

One and two and male and female,
they moved.
And God never seemed so real,
or so close,
and so inviting.

She was *God.*
And she ROCKED Nike Airs.

And I will never forget her.

Episode 3:

"My love anoints all ya joints and erogenous points..."

—Be With You Remix,
Lauryn Hill and Mary J. Blige
(1994)

He Compared Me to Water

He compared me to water -
a freeze-frame image that he'd seen once
in a book of African wonders.

He compared me to *water* -

The continuity of my spirit,
Calm ripples in the tide of my voice,
The fluidity of melon-ated skin,

Crashing   when   walk.
    waves   I

An unprecedented cool, Refreshing.
    water.

I folded his sincere metaphor tightly and
    tucked
    it
    away
Between the hidden spaces of my amygdala.
And I was *affected*.
Your metaphor was lost in a high tide in my bloodstream
And storm waters carried it away to pulsating tributaries
and trickling waterfalls.

You are indigo and silver,
    and nighttime will not let me forget you.
So here I am, *running* water...

Feeling a bit like **SHIFT**
                    ING air,
in search of your metaphor.
Curious about your bloodlines
and the origins of your Spirit.

If I am water, then you are Earth
and I *nourished* you into being.
And if you trace the bloodlines closely,
you would probably remember me.
I *was* the Oshun River from which you gathered water
for your offerings.
I *was* the sacred stream in which you were baptized.

Do you not recall?

    Is my touch not peculiarly familiar?

        Remember when the sun felt warm
        on our skin
        and we feasted on pounded yam
        and ripe melons?

And we bathed in the very waters that captivated
        you in that book of African wonders.

    And has my voice not always resonated
    in your Spirit and matched the vibration of
                        water?

Lie in the stillness of my night
and   *motion*

     constant   *of my tide.*

And by morning,
if *yet still* you do not remember me,
I will whisper it to you,

And you will *never* forget again.

Cobwebs;
An Unprecedented Love Affair

He kissed the cobwebs off my cheeks
And dust mites off my lips,
Caressed the *arches* of my feet
and contours of my hips.
He sipped the D
        R
          I
            P
              S of honeysuckle fingertips

And we tripped...and fell into a
        vortex of irresponsibility.

We were *engulfed* in flames and wildfires...
Smokey the Bear would've been concerned.
Bodies melted and spirits burned;
We turned time into gold.

I was *Rumpelstiltskin,*
     and he understood my alchemy.
And it seemed as though he worshipped me,
I wondered who he thought I was to wash and kiss my feet,
Like the apostles did *Yeshua,*
His Imperial Majesty.

My King, he *must* have recognized Divinity in me.
And in *him* I saw a solar god
and astral deities.

He had the kind of love that *empowered* me.

So when I shoot for the moon,
the stars just won't do
Because he's a Universe of possibilities...
He embodies Earth's Truth.

    Love is *you*.

A Long-Distance Love-Mesh

He sang me into an orgasm
That rumbled the earth's core
And shift
    ed tectonic plates.
His voice soothed and excited my
neurotransmitters
And inspired anxious cell structures to release
Liquid dopamine that s
        e
         e
       p
       e
      d
    from my Unmentionables
        by the barrel.
He felt my **eRupTions** across an imaginary chasm
That divides our physical selves.
We aimed for fleeting gratification,
But were surprised to be edified by an act that
We had clearly been doing *wrong* for far too long!

I uttered sacred sounds that filled the stratosphere,
And he demonstrated the kind of Reciprocity
    That a sista could get used.
Bringing me closer to a state of alt**ered**
consciousness…
There was me, there was he,
And the Womb that nourished us into being
And sustains us in our growth…

So I couldn't help feeling like my search for everlasting life
Had ended within this space,
Because my twenty second ascension to ethereal realms
Seemed to stretch into eternity in both directions...
In one direction, we were wed in the ancient city of
    Ile Ife
2000 years before the common era....
In the other direction, he sang me lullabies in Heaven
Until Paradise was restored on earth...
Our energy is ancient,
    familiar,
        and as potent as Mama's sweet tea at
        Sunday dinner.
He felt me from the inside-in,
Traveled through my bloodstream,
And rushed toward my heart to lock himself in its inner chamber.
He re-wired the circuit to respond to his energy field,
    and his alone.
My release of liquid dopamine was no coincidence,
For the Womb that nourished Us
Provided all that was necessary to shift tectonic plates
With only our bare hands...

    with only our bare hands...

An unprecedented potency.

I turned and
        arched
                my
                backside
              into
              his
                Spirit
To be held for the night,
And when I felt his arms reach across the imaginary chasm
That divides our physical selves to wipe the single tear
That fell in exuberance,
I *knew* that he was real.
And it was then that I prepared myself for a beautiful birth
From the womb that nourished us.

Where I *Cum* From:
On Orgasms and Origins

I *cum* from a place that is uncommon and
unconventional -
Something like an ether, the way the
hot gasses and flames amass
To later **e x p l ode** matter into **s p a ce**
like broken shards of glass.

Where I *cum* from is a sacred place,
A place that beckons to be worshipped
and forces into submission.
The Yoruba call it
      Inu,
Some call it the seat of the soul,
Some say the Womb of Yeye -
The source of intuition,
an infernal abyss.

I *cum* from the roots of Amarata trees
buried deep in **streaming** basins of moisture.
Where I *cum* from does not exist within the
confines of perception;
It can only be accessed in a Trance-like state,
induced by heavy breathing
at a metronomic pace,
One in which I hear the voices of the *Most High*
    and elevated ancestors.
Surely, I can never forget where I *cum* from
because it is an ancient space
that bears the footprints of souls who have *seen* the
light

And traveled *with* me to the mountaintop -
    In this life and the last.
Where I *cum* from is a tightly compacted
    ball of matter,
energy that anxiously fills the stratosphere
    and gets lost in lunar tides.
Where I *cum* from
    is a place where spirit dwells,
      a place where we openly engage in a
      dialogical discourse.
Bits of Heaven fall into my sacred ether
and I get to experience an aspect of His ecstasy
in the place where I *cum* from.
I transcend the physical plane
And provide the metaphysical a material existence
in this place
    where I *cum* from.
Where I *cum* from,
my Blackness
    Can
    neither
    be
    ignored,
    nor
    negated,
for I *cum* with an inescapable **r.h.y.t.h.m.** -
from an insurmountable depth.
Where I *cum* from is a culmination
of Taino,
    Amerindian,
  Yoruba,
    Seminole,

Cherokee,
    and Congolese
    drum calls
that invoke warrior spirits and compliment tribal dances.
Where I *cum* from
Cannot be seen with the naked eye,
but rather *experienced* through the
             naked self-
Two bare souls weighed against the feather of
MAAT -
Where I *cum* from is a place of Truth, Justice, and Righteousness.

I *cum* with the **wisdom** of those past,
the **knowledge** of those coming,
and the **passion** of strong winds.
I *cum* with the **THUNDER** of mother elephants running to save the dying child.

See, I know that my *cumming*
has nothing to do with simple pleasures.
And I overstand that when I *cum*,
My individual journey to the mountaintop is
        irrelevant
because where I *cum* from,
The only language that is spoken is
PURPOSE.

And I pray that you never forget
Where you
cum
from.

An Ethereal Threesome

"That's why, darling,
It's incredible that someone so unforgettable
Thinks that I am unforgettable too..."
         (*Unforgettable*, Nat King Cole)

> ...And it's amazing how the idea of a *You*
> and *Me* in the same life-long sentence
> *simultaneously*
> Has me thanking God more frequently,
> Acknowledging His power more
> eloquently,
> Bearing my soul, and re-defining intimacy...

Indeed we are involved in a *perpetual* three-some,
Some may call it freaky,

**But ain't no point in tryin' to get me some
If God can't have some *too*...**

See, the God between us
 makes
our
love
worth
making,

And if we keep to pleasing Him,
There won't be a need for fakin'
or falsely climaxxin'...
Because volcanic eruptions *can't compare* to
Orgasms that *God* inspires...

I now know that **the same** God that created these fires
within the Earth's core
Is **the same** God that's got me beggin' you for more,
the One who lies at the apex of this complex love triangle...

Brotha,
I'm
  feelin'
    you...

but I'm feelin' *Him* too…

And I don't see why I should choose 'cause
He makes this love thang better.

It's the God within you that's got me getting wetter
Than yo' childhood Slip n' Slide...
Let's take this ride,
Let's let *God* drive,
And we relax,
enjoyin' the diamond in the back
of this '83 Cadillac.

We can ride into the sunset of our lives
And take our last breath in each other's arms...
Allow Spirit to cradle us
until we are reborn
And find each other once again,
      Perhaps as adolescent friends...

And start the journey over,
      Make the Cadi *corner-bend.*

...Me and God sometimes share gossip,
And He said you were a keeper,
So I'm puttin' my last dollar into getting to go

D
E
E
P
er
With my partners in this three-some...
Once you've pleased God,

then I want *ME* some.

She's Infatuated with Satin

She's infatuated with *Satin*...

Caresses her lips,
    puckers and smiles.
Remembers the way it
encourages her sensibilities,
    Inspires her to *feel*.

She remembers tenderness...
Satin has a way of penetrating force-fields,
    De . con . struct . ing barriers,

    forcing you to feel *admired*.
Satin knows how to *appreciate* a woman –
It holds her in high regard.

She remembers Satin in retrospect.
Emotionless expressions reflect her longing -
Reminiscing about what was and *could've* been,
But will never be again.

Satin... had charm and charisma,
Sweeps millipedes off ALL its feet.
It's passive-aggressive –
    controls you from the inside-out.
It influences,
    but does not force.
It speaks,
    but does not retort.
Causes a calm excitement-
    category 1 tornadoes within her spirit.

It was like that *every* time Satin was around,
And every time Satin was *not* around.

Satin has a way of forcing you to remember,
And *refusing* to forget.
The memory is painful,
but sweet like
      buttercream.
Satin...causes a sort of conflict between
Mind   and   heart –
Leaves you hopelessly enraged and

     beautifully encouraged.

Satin *knows*...

Satin knows its power
And lives with *purpose.*
Changes every life it touches,
     and touches every life it can.
...made her spin silk webs just to say that it is
Satin,
And *silk just won't do.*
Has a way of making her feel inadequate,
Repressing, yet re-enforcing her greatness.
You see, Satin knows its worth
And only seeks the *worthy.*
Satin makes you feel blessed,
              and cursed...

She prays to lift the hex and retain the memory;
It hurts to remember,
        and worse to forget...

She settles for cotton -
Prays its *Satin-like* qualities into existence;

Spins silk webs,
And remembers that they *just won't do.*

Cries over crushed velvet...
Gazes at gossamer.

Satin seeks its next worthy victim,
    Takes bubble-baths with thorn-less roses.

But..

 Satin knows *Champagne,*
And he will never forget the taste of
Elegance
    Dedication,

        Higher
    And   Purpose.

...I remember you.

Love Harder

Persistent whispers –
    "Love, take me away."
Cleansed my body with black soap,
Black soap
    on
    Brown
    skin,
Brown fingertips
        E x t e n d e d to please,
    And purify,
    And pacify.
    He's peace.
        We pray.
The incense burnings are **thick**,
And time is of no consequence.
Took tastes of Nature's nectar,
And my, was it sweet!
    Wrapped in roses,
    Engulfed in flames,
fire-flight from phallic formations,
Locked in a luxurious Love-mesh.
And how quickly I forgot
Where I ended and you *began*…

Bold, Black sea
    like night.
We ebbed and *flowed*,
Followed the gravitational   L of the moon.
                  L
                  U
                  P

We promote and preserve procreation.
And here lies the love-child, and indeed
He is Black.
And Beautiful.
And **Bold**.
And Blessed.

We ask to be kept.
Preserve Preservation.
Seek Freedom.
and
        Love
      HARDER.

Episode 4:

"My Umi said shine your light on the world, Shine your light for the world to see..."

— *Umi Says*, Mos Def (1999)

Surrender

GUNPOWDER sitting in the pit of my stomach,
I keep wondering why I didn't know better,
or rather do better
Because I knew better.
So now I face retrogression,
I curl back into the belly-button
      from which I emerged
          and am **UN-**
              BORN.
Footsteps backward in darkness,
I remember light, but cannot touch it,
feel it illuminate my small and large intestine and
travel u
     p
     w
     a
     r
     d
         through the esophagus and out my mouth.
                    My words are *dim*;
          Shadows of an understanding
                        gone wrong.

Absence manifested,
For energy can neither be created,
     nor destroyed.

I have always been, and will always be,
But I have not always cried...

I imagine that I was a **BOULDER** once,
Or a crater on the moon,
Laughing haughtily at the **faulty impact** of comets
Who DARED to test my strength!

I stood **erect** in the face of danger and possibility,
And now pools of liquid sodium
Bolt unmoving ankles to the ground like
Ships
        docked at sea.
But my heart is **wavering** like
The white flag of surrender
on enemy grounds.

Looking in the recent past
to understand this present,
I am clear that CLARITY *is expensive*,
And comes at the cost of sacrifice and sobriety.

Indeed, if I encouraged my ~~kundalini~~ like the
Serpent under my heel
I would have had the energy to combat
the barrage of meteorites headed Northwest…
And if I were *very* brave,
        I would have predicted their coming.

**Sometimes we know, and we both
celebrate** AND **reject our knowing,**

Something like residing in coastal areas when
The prophets have disclosed
that the next natural disaster
Shall occur via the *waters*.

DIDACTIC DOPAMINE

I stayed on the coast,
And was

WASHED AWAY

by the tide.

I swallowed the **GUNPOWDER**,
And subjected myself to this fate.

I e x p l o de.

Please respectfully b
                U
                         r y   my ashes

Under the white flag of surrender.

It is through *God* that I am eternal,
So as my flesh erodes,
I pray that *She* cradle me into a time
When I may know life again,
And this time…

    ***act* upon my knowing.**

Retribution through Rebirth

I've been contemplating *suicide*...
A means by which to obtain the peace
 that I once had but can't remember.
Rusty nails bolting weary ankles
to hardwood floors
Desperately pleading **"EMANCIPATION!"**

Hung my wings up to dry next to the
                        white dress
      That I was baptized in.

And as I die,
I reintegrate myself into the Circle of Life
         unbroken.
But as for me, the ceaseless circling stops here.
No more spinnin' like grocery bags and windy
         days.
Even quantum singularities evolve...
A one dimensional material existence was never
         meant for me,
So I commit myself to the Earth from which I came
To be **REMOLDED** and allow God
To blow life into my second chance.
I've been contemplating suicide
And wondering if I'll be forgiven
For not doing so sooner.
               I am Spiritual mincemeat
                Anticipating a death in
           which I can actively participate –
               The agent of my own demise.

Judge me if you deem it appropriate
But know that submitting to the will of anyone
Except the Most High is suicide *epitomized.*
So take heed to the four fingers pointing
    Back at you.
And sincerely ask yourselves if perhaps
you are dead
already.

Hung my wings up to dry next to the
                     white dress
    That I was baptized in.

Daddy, would you do me the honor
Of giving me away to the Earth that birthed me
And the sea that cradled me.
Sprinkle my ashes over the *Nile,*
But do so sparingly.
        And watch closely as the
        "me" that was
        ushers in a new beginning.
Saturn is calling for me to hang about its rings
Because the Earth can't hold me anymore.
And woe upon he that attempts to hinder my
liberation
Because he ain't brave enough to seek his own!

Brother,
pass me my wings off that clothesline there!

And in the likely event of my demise,
Thank the High Heavens and celebrate
my new beginning. Ashe.

Phyl•liz Sóph°i'kăl
the Phonetician

La Brea:
In Reverence of the Souls at Pitch Lake

I took my shoes off to reverence them,
Those Ancestral Spirits
ceremonially cast into the S
                          I
                          N
                          K
                          I
                          N
                          G   deep.
A fluid abyss,
   blacker than the skies at midnight
        welcomed them,
And I trusted their protection.
They call them Carib and Arawak,
but perhaps they called *themselves*

Daughter, Son, Mother, Father, and

children of the Sky and Earth.

                    They dwelled there,
          subtly making their presence known
                  to those who chose
                      AWARENESS.

They spoke in bubbles that
        sprang up
from gaseous spaces within the cor e.

They spoke of war,
               changes,
           choices,
               and
                   REMEMBERING...
And they blessed me with gifts
that carried the essence of lives past
and lives to come.
                 They asked to be known intimately
                 and never forgotten -
Because whether the **LEGENDS** be
     Truth or Fiction,
The voices of those cast into the sinking deep
can never be denied.

They will call, and call,
and await the recognition of those who have come
seeking pretty pictures and nice stories.
But to those who listen, and subsequently hear,
the surface is *least* appealing.

It is what lies *deep*
that integrates the individual self
into the greater whole.
                      And THAT is all that matters...
Because Mother Hummingbird
was cast into the sinking deep,
and Father Raven
was sent on a trail of tears to Oklahoma,
                           And now,
      Sons and Daughters of the sinking deep
            and tear-stained trails
     Must take off their shoes in reverence.

Because War, too, is Sacred

Sacred herbs in a calabash...

Contagious chants and
      r.h.y.t.h.m.i.c. dances
invoke the ancient warriors
who come to fight alongside
            face paint and feathers,
                      Fire and fury.

Restless rage grounded in
         Divine Ordinances,
SHAKING SPEARS
and flames that b
           o
              w   in reverence...

The battle is long, and the buffalo grow tired,
    The corn is uninspired,
    and the potatoes, apathetic.
Weary seasons are reluctant to come,
And trampled soil threatens survival.

Time is tender...

            And lunar tides remind them that
            the Earth is ceaselessly in motion.

The sun greets them at daybreak
with javelins and pierced hearts,
And the **overnight ambush** is merciless.

The opponents have invaded the camp
and violated a rare serenity;
Interrupted dreams of peaceful negotiations.

The waves are crashing violently now,
For the war has endured far too long,
And the warriors have forgotten that
all things have its time -

Time is tender...

But the victorious ones have
   REMEMBERED
    THEIR
     DEITIES,
**they have
danced and prayed
before battle,**
        **they have
    called on the energy of sky and Earth,
     of water and fire.**
   and they have fed their ancestors.

They have remembered that
war, too, is sacred,
And they carry the calabash
      alongside the *SHAKING SPEAR*.

Sons and daughters of the Universe do not march;

They are **CARRIED** to victory.

In the Center of my Lotus

Will you be the Jewel
      in the Center of my
           Lotus,
The diamond in the midst of my rough dreams,
The treasure b
        u
          r
                ied deep in troubled waters,
        Receptor of projected light beams?

Will you be still with me
long enough to hear the voice of *God*
e c h o through Eternity in
    both directions,
and back to this present moment
              which always was and
              shall forever be?

Will you be the jewel
      in the center of my
           Lotus -
The rock that bears a **bold** bosom to the M
                    O
                    O
                    N.
Will you sit with me in perfect stillness, and know?
Know that my melanin is adequate,
and it makes me **fully human**
      and **fully God**
           at the same time.

Will you sit with me in perfect stillness and know
that **each** time we sit in **perfect stillness,**
The *Messiah* returns.

Will you sit with me in overstanding
    that we are
    sons and daughters
    of a Spirit that has
    commissioned us with PURPOSE?

We are OUR OWN redeemers,
                  When will we know?

Will you be the jewel
    in the center of my
        Lotus?
And look in **perfect stillness** at the stars,
    and know -
Know that we are composed of bits of stardust,
And we are made to be
    Brilliant.
        Inspiring.
            Infinite.
                    Timeless.
They forgot to tell you that
comets have melanin, too.
              When will we know?
They forgot to tell you that we are *infinite*,
And the only thing that limits us is
        limited consciousness.
And if we stop *doing* long enough to *BE*,
far greater things are accomplished.

Can we acknowledge

that we are microcosmic
      and MACROCOSMIC
    at the *same time?*
               When will we know?
When will we know that
    we are **more** than the iceberg's tip?
Will you be the jewel
      in the center of my
           Lotus?
Will you walk with me to Kilimanjaro and witness
One million melanated people
            Move a mountain with their minds?
Will you not be surprised?
Will you know that such a feat reflects
The *least* of our capabilities?
      If only we resurrected the jewels
        lying dormant in our Lotuses...
If all melanated people told the Red Sea to part,
               it would listen.

When will we know that we are Moses?
And that WE ARE ALL EACH OTHER'S WAY

    to DIAMOND existences.
and our jewels are the keys to our overstanding.
We must sit in perfect stillness before we can move,
So will you be the jewel
      in the center of my
           Lotus?
                Will you be still, be still and
        KNOW THAT YOU ARE GOD.

I Am Balance (A Meditation)

I am Balance.

I am the lava that runs thru the core of the Earth,
I am igneous rock.
I am the temptation at the base of the volcano,
I am Sandalwood, I am Saturn and SHANGO,
I am the foundation, I am secure,
I am bloodstone, ruby, and hematite.
I am **Red**.

I am sensual, I am desirable.
I am Salsa.
I am oranges and Jasmine oil,
I am Sensation, I am Water,
I am Yoga, I am Yemoja,
I am Jupiter and Scorpio, Svadisthana,
I am a pyramid,
I am Carnelian and Onyx,
I am **Orange**.

I am a lustrous jewel,
I am E major,
I am vision,
I am grapefruit,
I am Mars,
I am Topaz and Citrine.
I am sunflowers.
I am lion, I am gold, I am warrior.
I am freedom, I am fire, I am Oshun.
I am **yellow**.

I am a crescent moon,
I am unstruck.
I am copper, I am a massage,
I am self-love, I am AIR,
I am periodot and sisterhood,
I am **Ogun**, I am Taurus,
I am Spain.
I am Foxglove and Carnation,
Anahata,
I am **green.**

I am Purification.
I am Mercury, I am Gardenia,
I am the opera,
I am Tai Chi,
I am the ethers,
I am an inverted pyramid,
I am OBATALA,
I am Blue Chamomile,
I am will and expression,
I am **Turquoise.**

I am a Mozart Sonata,
I am the Cosmos,
I am control and Wisdom,
I am Peru.
I am Camphor oil and Sapphire,
I am the moon.
I am Ajna, I am Pisces,
I am discernment, **ORUNMILA**, and Lapis Lazuli,
I am **Indigo.**

I am thousand-fold.
I am Spiritual Understanding,
I am Aquarius,
I am the Lotus Flower,
I am Grace and Serenity,
I am self-less,
I am meditation,
I am Amethyst and *Platinum*,
I am stillness,
I am Ori,
I am **violet.**

Ashe.

First Poem in Dedication to *you*

It's the kind of butterflies
you get in the sixth grade,
And you can't sleep because you can't wait
to see him the next day.
                It's "first day of kindergarten" nervous,
It's "Mama's gonna beat me" scared,
            It's "dancing in the pew" exciting,
It's "raise my hands in exaltation" amazing,
            It's "bow my head in reverence" humbling...

And I pray that rivers of peace and tranquility
Are ushered in soon
Because I can't sleep,
And I'm so nervous.
And I'm thinking about you.
And I pray that rivers' tributaries
Usher in humble beginnings

For **we**, who give **you** life,

And **you**, who give **us**

ETERNITY.

Your journey is *Divinely Sanctioned,*
And ours is just beginning.
Trust the river that will guide you to my arms,
And I will do the same.
Come forth, oh Ancestor Angel;

           You were created from love.

Daughter of two Mothers

I am the daughter of

the 4 cardinal directions
and the waters

Of the herbs
and the palm oil,

of the teepee
and the hut.

I am the daughter of
two mothers,
the daughter of
two legacies.

                    I suckled at two breasts,
                    emerged from two wombs,
                    and indeed,

I levitated.

I AM NOT A BASTARD CHILD.

Dedicated to the Big Bang

I heard her whisper that
one flew over the coocoo's nest,
And I shuddered to think that God's work could be
criticized in such a fashion.
>But I never promised you a rose garden,
>And you never promised me
>words like honey dew melons.

You never promised me a world without judgment,
>and neither did the *Most High*.

It was prophesied that the righteous would be
condemned for *His* name's sake,

But what about *Hers*?
The rainbow
 never promised that it would never rain,
And the serpent
never agreed to try to walk again.

>**So here I am,**
>
>**Just as I was yesterday,**
>
>**and so shall I be tomorrow,**

Perhaps slightly more evolved,
Yet still simply an outgrowth of the blastocyst
that was attached to the uterine wall.
I am a product of my environment;
that is without question.

>My blood is a river,
>My arms are branches,
>My feet are boulders,
>My nose is a pyramid,

My eyes are quantum singularities,
My mouth is a cave,
My neck is a waterfall, my hair -
A field of buttercups,
My womb, *the Big Bang.*

And here I am,

Just as I was yesterday,

and so shall I be tomorrow —
An outgrowth of the blastocyst
attached to the uterine wall.

And I do not owe it to you to return to Heaven and
choose a different fate.
I do not owe it to you to reverse the process of my
Growth for your convenience.
I do not owe it to you to become who I never was
in order to soothe your soul.
I do not owe it to you to relinquish my Freedom to
live in the cage your mind has created for me.
I do not owe it to you to deny Them
simply because you won't look back.

But when the scenery around you has changed,
And the transition has commenced –
When you *become* the breeze that causes
the buttercups to sway –
When you *become* the current in the river–
When you *become* the Black of the Berry
and the sweetness in its juice –

When you realize that you are both
Spirit and Earth –
When you *become* the dust, the earthen
red clay,
The quartz crystal or the blue sapphire,
When you are thirsty, and need a drink of
cool water –
You would want me to remember you...

And I shall,
Because after all,
I am a product of my environment –
An outgrowth of the blastocyst attached to the
uterine wall.
I am here because of YOU,
And you must realize that
your womb is too
the Big Bang.

You were commissioned,

and here I am.

Just as I was yesterday,

and so shall I be tomorrow –

The star that was implanted

in *your* universe...

Please forgive me for being Nibiru,
I'm not the SATURN you expected.

ABOUT THE AUTHOR

I was born in Fort Lauderdale, Florida and relocated to Atlanta, Georgia during my adolescent years. After completing a Bachelor of Arts in African-American Studies (Concentration in Social-Behavioral Sciences) with a minor in Spanish, I went on to obtain a Master of Arts in Pan-African Studies and a Graduate Certificate in Women and Gender Studies.

My life has been a process of acquiring the knowledge, insight, and experience to produce substantial, thought-provoking, and transformative work, in an effort to touch and heal the hearts of nations.

My passion for education, the arts, Hip-Hop, and the youth traverse every area of my life, and each one significantly impacts my artistic and professional endeavors.

It is my hope that this work is refreshing and edifying, and I personally thank you for your support and the energy that you have invested in engaging my words. I look forward to your support on future projects!

www.ingramcontent.com/pod-product-compliance
Lightning Source LLC
Chambersburg PA
CBHW071721040426
42446CB00011B/2158